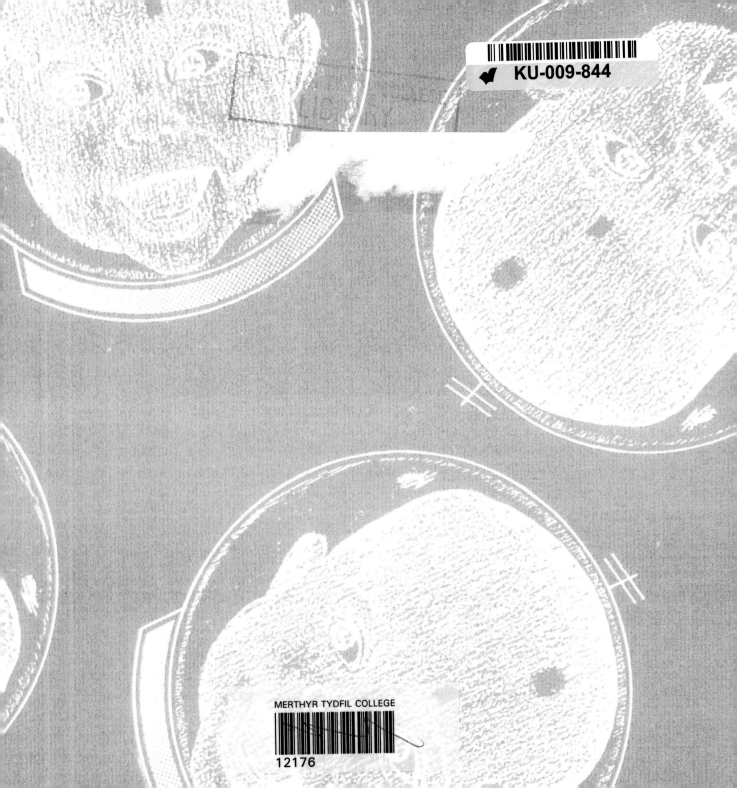

KU-009-844

Red or Dead

Wayne
Hen

TAMSIN KINGSWELL

Red or Dead

The Good, the Bad,
and the Ugly

WATSON-GUPTILL
PUBLICATIONS
New York

First published in 1998 in the United States of America
by Watson-Guptill Publications, a division of
BPI Communications, Inc.,
1515 Broadway, New York, NY 10036

Library of Congress Catalog Card Number: 98-86821

ISBN 0-8230-1204-2

This book was conceived,
designed, and produced by
THE IVY PRESS LTD
2/3 St Andrews Place
Lewes
East Sussex BN7 1UP

Art Director: Terry Jeavons
Design and page layout: Harry Green
Commissioning Editor: Christine Davis
Editorial Director: Sophie Collins

Printed in Hong Kong

Contents

In the making of this book I have had to look at the whole visual history of Red or Dead—the good, the bad, and the ugly. I have had to revisit past collections, political stances, and philosophies, and I wouldn't change a thing. We have had to struggle against a designer industry steeped in elitism, but the barriers are coming down. We are proving that it is still possible to create valuable brands using youthful energy and human values. I am proud of Red or Dead, what it stands for, and the impact it is having on the concept of designer fashion. This is only just the beginning; we are going to make a lasting difference."

Wayne Hemingway

Introduction

PEOPLE HAVE ALWAYS found Red or Dead hard to define. A high-fashion collection at affordable prices, a label without a designer's name attached, with its roots in secondhand clothes stalls and flea markets rather than pattern-cutting and Paris. And at the center, Wayne Hemingway, a man who doesn't draw, yet manages to embrace the mood of the moment with unnerving accuracy.

Red or Dead has always been less a label for a label's sake and more a vehicle for Hemingway's convictions on everything from fashion to nuclear testing. "Innovative, challenging fashion at an accessible level," reads the company's mission statement. Red or Dead turns established preconceptions about fashion on their head, making the uncool cool, saying the unsayable. Hemingway may sound idealistic when talking about his beliefs and his label, but it is his clarity of vision that has made Red or Dead so popular. Put simply, he has managed to embody the ideology of British youth culture. "The philosophy of Red or Dead comes from my belief that design and fashion shouldn't be only for the rich. Today the whole population is bombarded by media, and people have developed a sense of style—something that was once the preserve of the few." Hemingway undoubtedly understands his market. "Being a teenager or in your early 20s is the best time for fashion. You've got the time, your mind is uncluttered, and you want to look your best because you want sex, you want to stand out. Young people today know about style, but haven't got the money to spend." Affordability, then, is key. "Our biggest achievement has been in making people realize that there is more to fashion than very expensive, art-inspired elitist clothing. We chipped away at the barrier, but we have only just begun to break it down."

Fashion addict

Family ties and formative influences run deep through Hemingway's collections. Even the name Red or Dead comes from his father, a Native American chief who met Hemingway's

"The philosophy of Red or Dead comes from my belief that design and fashion shouldn't be only for the rich."

Below: The distinctive Red or Dead logo, inspired by Russian Constructivist imagery.

Right: Red or Dead's point-of-sale material draws on kitsch images, often found at flea markets.

mother in Morecambe, England. The northern seaside town had yet to become the kitsch epicenter it is today, and in the 1950s and 60s it had a strong youth culture. "Looking back, fashion was a really major thing in our household. My mum, my nan, and my granddad were so cool. My mum's had a big influence on my life. At home she was always making clothes, buying the latest patterns from Vogue and Biba—she must have been their biggest mail-order customer. When I look at pictures of Mum, she was the original walking, talking fashion victim. My nan was the same. They even dressed me up—I was like a little doll. One week I was Elvis, the next I was one of the Beatles, and then I'm a bloody body-builder with a Tarzan outfit pushing a little cart of bricks."

Dressing up became a code to live by, an expression of individuality. "At school I was always the one in trouble for messing around with the uniform. First the trousers had to be flares [bell-bottoms] and then they had to be 'Bowie' trousers. The shoes had to be either brothel creepers [crêpe-soled suede shoes] or winkle pickers [pointed shoes], whatever I could get hold of." Despite these seminal influences, fashion wasn't an early career dream; with Hemingway, it was always music first. By the age of 13 he was a regular club-goer, cutting his teeth on Northern Soul at the casino in Wigan. The whole scene had a profound effect. "It was partly the music, but it was also the fashion side—it was a style, almost a tribal thing. Your trousers had to be a certain width with so many pockets on them, your shoes had to be a certain type, you had to tuck your beer towel in your trousers and the badges had to be sewn on in the right places."

By the time he was 16, Hemingway had ceased to be a soul-boy, falling instead for the lure of punk. "Punk happened when I was still at school, it just hit me and I thought, this is for me. The Sex Pistols played Blackburn, of all places. The whole ethos of punk appealed to Hemingway. "This was proper rebellion—it was everything that being young was supposed to be about: the self-expression, the D.I.Y. [do-it-yourself] ethic, the energy."

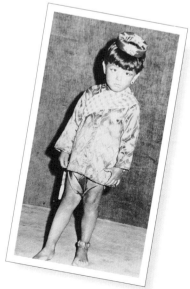

Left: Lineup for the spring/summer 1996 catwalk.

Below: Hemingway the nascent fashion victim, aged three.

The concept behind Red or Dead can be pinpointed to a trip to London. "I can remember this vividly, going down to London with some mates; we all knew what we wanted to do—walk down the King's Road and buy clothes from Vivienne Westwood's Seditionaries store. But when we got in the door we were stunned. Everything was there, including the T-shirts Johnny Rotten was wearing, but they cost about £50. I felt so betrayed. I thought, 'This isn't what punk is supposed to be—it's just middle-class people wearing expensive clothes.' The philosophy behind punk was right: it was all about cutting through class barriers, bringing a youth movement and fashion within reach of everybody. I was totally disillusioned. I wanted to go back with bags laden with clothes, but I couldn't afford anything."

Instead of giving up on punk, Hemingway decided to channel this disappointment into putting looks together, bastardizing, raiding old footwear warehouses for ancient brothel creepers, and digging around the secondhand shops that had just begun opening in Manchester, for things like nylon bathrobes. "I started experimenting like mad with clothes. It was basically a D.I.Y. attitude—that was what punk was supposed to be about. I decided to leave it to the plastic punks in London to spend a fortune on T-shirts; I was going to do it my own way."

Hitting the streets

At 18, Hemingway decided to give London a go and went to University College there to study for a B.S. in geography and meteorology. Music was still a major force in his life, with punk giving way to rockabilly and the New Romantics. Hemingway enthusiastically embraced the club and street culture that had blossomed in the early 1980s. It was a busy time: Hemingway became a DJ, toured with Dexy's Midnight Runners, formed a band, ran a club, and met his future wife and business partner, Gerardine. "She was an avid clothes maker and I was a avid clothes collector. She'd be making outfits all week to wear for clubbing at the weekend."

Above: Early days at Camden Market.

Right: The New Romantic influence: shirt from spring/summer 1989.

"Punk was proper rebellion—it was everything that being young was supposed to be about."

10

Camden Market, in north London, was Hemingway's big break into the world of fashion. Camden in the early 1980s was at the heart of London cool, but Hemingway's involvement was driven more by necessity than by a love of clothing design. "We needed some money to pay the rent and also needed to buy lots of equipment for the band. Gerardine had all these clothes that she had made, so we put them in a market stall, along with clothes that I'd collected, and it worked. We made £80 in one go, and the rent was about £6. We did it every week, and before we knew it we had 16 stalls. I was going to jumble sales, car-boot sales, Oxfam shops, everywhere, buying clothes for 10p and selling them for £10, easy. I never thought it would last—I saw it as a lucrative sideline, really." It was also an education. "I possibly learned just as much about the history of clothing as I would have done by studying design in college. By that time we were even importing to keep up with demand—I was buying from Europe and America. We definitely became the biggest secondhand people in London. We were selling clothes to Japan, and people were coming from all over to buy them. If I hadn't got a bit bored with it, I'm sure we'd still be making money out of it now."

Gerardine's own collection, meanwhile, was on sale in London's Kensington Market, at that time a center of young fashion. As ever, the Hemingways were in the right place at the right time—and doing the right thing. The U.S. department store Macy's visited the market to get a feel for English street fashion and promptly ordered 200 pieces from the collection. Hemingway roped in his mother to run a small factory in the north and started manufacturing the clothes. Red or Dead was officially born.

Success story
The leap to big-time success, however, came in the unlikely shape of a previously ignored workwear sole. Hemingway put Dr. Martens on the map and they went on to become the footwear fashion phenomenon of the 1980s. "That was perfect timing.

Red or Dead scored early success with shoe designs.

Right: Slip-on with "69" logo, 1987.

Below: Camouflage wing-back, 1989.

"Everybody wanted Dr. Martens—

Jean-Paul Gaultier, Demi Moore,

and every star you could think of."

Left: Plastic Union Jack slip-on, 1989.

Right: square-toed boot, 1988.

There were all these girls wearing tight black dresses and high heels, and we changed the silhouette by putting a bloody big pair of boots at the end. Then everybody wanted them—Jean-Paul Gaultier was buying them from our stall in Camden, Demi Moore, and every star you could think of, it was unbelievable." Spotting a lucrative partnership, Hemingway worked with Dr. Martens, designing and exporting for the company, and all the while making a stockpile of cash that in due course enabled him to fund the launch of Red or Dead as a fashion label in its own right. "We didn't need financial backing from banks at that stage to get us off the ground. We had Dr. Martens and secondhand clothes as our benefactors."

Hemingway followed with an own-label range of shoes, and in 1986 opened Red or Dead's first shop, in Rupert Street in London's Soho. Clothing followed in 1987, with a move to a larger site in Covent Garden's Neal Street. Retail expansion was always a vital part of the plan. "You can get your message across in your own shop—you don't have to rely on buyers, who are traditionally very conservative. We can take risks, because it's our own collection." The first shop interiors reflected Red or Dead's own values, with everything made from recycled materials but utilized in an inventive, modern way. This idiosyncratic stance continues today. "We have always used fashion style no-nos, like stone cladding and pebble dashing. You wouldn't put all that stuff in a fashion shop normally, but it's perfect for Red or Dead."

As always, the timing was just right. "Neal Street was on the verge of becoming a fashion mecca and was attracting high-profile fashion-conscious figures such as the Pet Shop Boys, Kylie Minogue, Jason Donovan, and, crucially, Bros. The Bros twins were *the* teen band of 1987 and were regularly kitted out at Red or Dead. The key feature of their wardrobe was the Watch shoe, an original Red or Dead design which featured a watch face mounted on the top of a ripple-soled black lace-up shoe. Bros wore them everywhere they went, and their fans flocked to Neal

"I decided to leave it to the plastic punks in London to spend a fortune on T-shirts; I was going to do it my own way."

Left: One of Red or Dead's first shops, in London's Neal Street.

Below: The Watch shoe as sported by the teen band Bros, 1987.

street to snap up a pair for themselves. We probably made as much money as Bros did—we couldn't keep up with the demand. On a Saturday morning the queues were so long we had to have bouncers on the door." The resulting healthy cash flow allowed for further expansion of the business, and enabled Hemingway to begin building his own team of designers.

Ten years on, Red or Dead employs 120 people and the company's retail base has grown to ten shops, including outlets in Prague and Tokyo, alongside, in England, Sheffield, Newcastle, Birmingham, Manchester, and Nottingham, as well as hundreds of other retailers worldwide. "Tokyo was an obvious choice: we have a massive distribution there with Japan's second-largest corporation. We also chose to go into Prague in 1998. We've got a very strong following in all those Eastern European markets. Some people make 'communist' associations with the name, which might have helped, but it's our philosophy which seems to really strike a chord with young people in these countries."

Hemingway doesn't shy away from lucrative tie-ins with mail-order companies, believing that accessibility in any form cannot be a bad thing. "We are not ashamed of the fact that you can buy Red or Dead in a Grattan catalog. As long as the product is good, as long as it carries our message, and as long as we're not ripping anyone off by just using our name, then that's fine. I would even talk to Woolworth's about stocking our clothes, if it could be done correctly, with our brand values upheld. It would be great to have Red or Dead next to the pick 'n' mix sweet counter!" Success in the fashion world, it seems, has not diminished Hemingway's anti-establishment stance: "I haven't got any time for that old-school preciousness and elitism. We are not just Wayne Hemingway, we are Red or Dead, and although we may initially have suffered as a result of people's preconceptions, we have so much more longevity. Red or Dead has a personality that the public can associate with. It doesn't belittle, rip off, or abuse its customers or status. The fact that we have human values makes us modern, and very relevant."

"I haven't got any time for that old-school preciousness and elitism. The fact that we have human values makes us modern, and very relevant."

Above: Swing tags from the spring/ summer 1998 collection, "Beautiful Freaks."

Left and far left: Playing with unexpected images, Hemingway uses a montage of Victorian dolls for a spring/summer 1992 print.

RED OR DEAD can be seen as the embodiment of British street culture, the ultimate street label. And Hemingway, always running as fast as he can in the opposite direction from the fashion establishment, has all the right credentials. Having started his company quite literally on the streets, he has immediate empathy with his young, street fashion–conscious customers.

"I always wanted to create a brand that summed up what British youth culture stood for. Why is it that we can do it with pop groups, but not with fashion? British music manages to reflect what's going on in the U.K., our lives, and the times we're living in. Fashion is just as important, but we've been hijacked by foreign brands. I'm quite patriotic; I've always known that a lot of the best ideas come out of Britain, but it seems to be other countries that go and make all the money.

"Street culture has had a huge influence on Red or Dead, but the relationship is not just one-way. We've also made street culture, probably more than any other designer label has done. When you look at some of our collections,

you can see just how far they were ahead of their time. We often do things first: Dr. Martens and big shoes; the Farah trouser; the E-generation slogan T-shirts; picking up on Indian influences way before anyone else did. What we are really good at is taking something that someone is wearing and going further with it. Often, the cultural mixes that you see around you—especially in places

"INDIAN SUMMER" COLLECTION
Spring/summer 1997

Drawing inspiration from the ethnic mix of London's streets, Red or Dead plays with the differing styles of contemporary British Asians.

like London—just trigger something off in your mind. If anything, we are one step ahead of the street, and that's why so many people like what we do.

"Our first catwalk collection was very much influenced by the street—even the Space Baby print. We were walking through Les Halles in Paris when we saw a girl dressed futuristically. I said, 'She's a real space baby.' Then we saw these postcards of babies, bought one, stuck a helmet round its head, and the Space Baby print was born. It was 1990, the turn of the decade, and it hit the right chord. Everyone bought the T-shirt, and everyone ripped it off. There was even a band called the Space Babies. When you look back now, the collection was quite naive, but it was so right for the time.

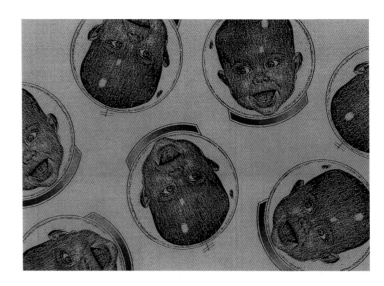

"SPACE BABY"
COLLECTION
Spring/summer 1990

Still the definitive Red or Dead print, the baby in a space helmet appeared on bags, shorts, halter tops, and even transparent Dr. Marten boots. The Space Baby wedding dress (*above center*) **is now in the Victoria & Albert Museum in London.**

15

"The street and music also affected Red or Dead's shoe design. We'd been experimenting with footwear for a while, looking at shoes that had been hijacked for street fashion. We'd popularized those black gym pumps [sneakers] that you'd wear at school. Then we imported Chinese slippers, Ian McCulloch of Echo and the Bunnymen–style shoes, which he used to wear with a long overcoat and woolly jumper [sweater], and the thinnest soled pumps that you could find. A lot of inspiration has come from music, especially punk and the music that started it—Iggy and the Stooges, the New York Dolls. Glam rock has also been a big influence. Things like tattoos and painted bodies have all come from the music scene.

INSPIRED BY MUSIC
Spring/summer 1995 and 1996

Hemingway's love affair with music has been a major influence on Red or Dead's collections—whether in the form of Glam rock–inspired body paint or an androgynous punk look (both 1996). The invitation for the spring/summer 1995 collection was a pastiche of heavy-metal band Motorhead's logo.

Red or Dead taps into
the harder edge of
popular culture and
street style.
Hemingway was
instrumental in the
punk revival and
has flirted with the
appeal of heavy
metal in his collections.

"We also targeted corporate logos. It was at the beginning of the Acid House thing and we did a T-shirt that took the piss out of [made fun of] E-speak [club talk]. It was a 'Hoover' logo but with 'Groover' written on it. We changed Lego to Redo, Jaffa to Naffa. Of course the brands objected, and we had to pull nearly all of them. The best one was a T-shirt with the Shell Oil logo, which we changed to 'Hell' in a link-up with Greenpeace. We really got into attacking the big corporations, and one by one they blasted us—but not before we got a lot out onto the marketplace. That really appealed to me. We were selling thousands of these subversive T-shirts. That's what our customers wanted to wear, not a posh dress on a catwalk. It was street fashion as I had always imagined it."

LOGO T-SHIRTS
Spring/summer 1991

Hemingway's impish sense of humor has caused several run-ins with the establishment. These styles had to be pulled from the shops when the various companies accused Red or Dead of undermining their branding.

19

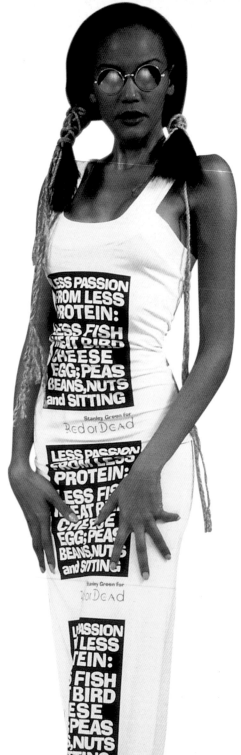

One of Hemingway's favorite English eccentrics was Stanley Green, an "old man who used to walk down Oxford Street with a big placard claiming that protein was the root of evil. I used to love seeing him and really liked his bit of political activism. He was about as much 'street' as you can possibly get . . .

"When we put cider bottles on the catwalk in 1993, it was our response to a fashion journalist who complained about street fashion. She said that it was terrible for the industry, that it was just scruffy and not what fashion was all about. Basically she was claiming that street fashion was fashion for down-and-outs—a really horrible comment. So we did a complete V sign up it [gave it the finger], putting models on the catwalk with cider bottles in their holsters and carrying copies of *The Big Issue* [a magazine sold by homeless people in the U.K.].

"Street fashion is a much-misunderstood concept; it is certainly not a word that I like to use regularly. But you can't escape from the fact that a walk through an urban center in the U.K. reveals an army of inspired young people, who in turn can be an inspiration to designers."

STANLEY GREEN
Spring/summer 1993

Stanley Green, an English eccentric who would make a daily pilgrimage up and down London's Oxford Street inspired Red or Dead's 1993 collection to immortalize Green's trademark "Eat Less Protein" placard.

"PLEASE DON'T PINCH"
Spring/summer 1996

Red or Dead's teasing
message on a micro
bikini, with its reference
to picture-postcard
sexuality, harks back
to Hemingway's
seaside upbringing
in Morecambe.

**GOLD LAMÉ
DRESS**
Spring/summer 1994

In a fusion of street and
high fashion, a slinky
gold dress is combined
with a punky hairstyle.

**CIDER ON THE
CATWALK**
Spring/summer 1993

Hemingway was dismayed
by a fashion journalist's
dismissal of street fashion.
He responded by sending
models down the catwalk
with cider bottles in
holsters and carrying
copies of *The Big Issue*
[a magazine sold by
homeless people in
the U.K.].

NOT FOR HEMINGWAY the elitist influences of fine art and theater—inspiration for Red or Dead prints and designs often comes from his passion for thrift shops and trunk sales. The flotsam and jetsam that people discard fascinates Hemingway, and has proved a rich source over the years. The walls of his office are covered with rummage sale finds, every available surface filled with glass animals, snow-scene paperweights, straw donkeys, and kitsch holiday souvenirs.

"I've always enjoyed finding funny things from thrift sales—it's really a hobby. In many of our collections there's been a print inspired by something I've found. The Wedgwood print came from a car-boot [trunk] sale find. Wedgwood china has to be one of the saddest things anybody could ever collect. Garden gnomes, too: we now have a fantastic gnome garden at home. You can also always find those pictures of doe-eyed little girls and boys. We've had T-shirts printed with them and they've sold really well, as has the artificial wood-grain print, taken from those 1960s Formica tables.

GNOME PRINT
Spring/summer 1994

Hemingway's yard at home is filled with gnomes, so it was only a matter of time before the bearded man with a pointy hat made an appearance on the Red or Dead catwalk.

POINT-OF-SALE
Fall/winter 1995

Wide-eyed children leaking tears may not win any prizes for good taste, but Red or Dead's point-of-sale cards elevate the images to an art form.

WEDGWOOD FROCKS
Spring/summer 1996

Hemingway cites the famous blue-and-white Wedgwood china as one of the saddest things anyone could collect. No surprises, then, that it ended up as a Red or Dead print.

FORMICA WOOD PRINT
Fall/winter 1994

Red or Dead turns a tacky print on its head by using it for a chic and sophisticated eveningwear look.

TCHECHNIKOV
PRINT
Fall/winter 1994

The "Blue Lady" had become a flea market special by the time Hemingway developed an interest in her kitsch appeal. When blown up, the portrait takes on an abstract quality that works well with its distinctive original coloring.

"Probably my favorite car-boot find of all time is the Tchechnikov Lady; she's also known as the Blue Lady, but can be brown or green as well! She sums up that naff [tacky] style of the 1960s and 70s—it's the archetype of what people with 'taste' wanted on their walls. I actually think those pictures are really beautiful, and they're collectable now. Things that come from car-boot sales aren't just kitsch. Look at the butterfly print we did, which was beautiful. That came from a kid's scrapbook of butterflies.

"Flight bags were massive for us; the concept was also taken up by Comme des Garçons, D&G [Dolce & Gabbana], all sorts of people. The heyday of flight bags and cruise bags was the 1960s and 70s. The first one I had was a present from my nan, a cruise bag. I just thought they were really funny, and I started collecting them. It was easy to find these bags because nobody ever wanted them; old men would carry their tools in them and keep them out in the shed.

"I'm really proud that we were able to take old 'genteel,' stuffy floral prints and recreate them for the 1998 spring/ summer collection. Remember Laura Ashley? It is so uncool; we had it in our house in the early 1980s, curtains with those little prints. I had played around with the idea for a while and managed to get hold of some early Laura Ashley dresses—they looked really good. It was time to make the uncool cool. So we researched it, found old catalogs, went to thrift sales. The collection was influenced by the idea rather than the actual designs. Could anyone else have thought of Laura Ashley as an inspiration?"

Hemingway's fascination with flight bags began at an early age and has since inspired one of Red or Dead's most successful accessories lines.

BUTTERFLY
PRINT
Spring/summer 1995

The butterfly print was a Red or Dead bestseller, and a timely reminder that the label was capable of far more than just shock tactics and street wear.

"BEAUTIFUL
FREAKS"
COLLECTION
Spring/summer 1998

Subverting one of British fashion's most traditional stalwarts, Red or Dead reinvents the Laura Ashley look.

Humor

ONE OF RED OR DEAD's design signatures is its use of humor and irony. It's a balance that has taken years to get right. Hemingway openly admits that in some collections the humor was applied too heavily and that even today he sometimes winces when he sees certain things come down the catwalk. But humor and irony remain integral to the Red or Dead label. From the very first show, Red or Dead catwalks were littered with subtle—and not-so-subtle—visual jokes: fur-trimmed diapers and bibs, bridal dresses made from discarded rubbish, pitbull terriers, stuffed donkeys, and Naomi Campbell's mother.

"I find humor, often too much humor, in everything. It's everyday humor, not high-brow stuff; the kind of comedians I like are Vic and Bob [Reeves and Mortimer], Dick Emery, Les Dawson, Tommy Cooper. Humor was a seminal influence in my youth and remains so today. It shouldn't be in absolutely everything Red or Dead does, but the second we lose our sense of humor and irony, we lose a really important element.

SYNTHETIC FUR
DRESS
Fall/winter 1995

Bright pink fun fur and a friendly pit bull terrier add a riot of color, and just a little bit of controversy, to Red or Dead's catwalk show.

BOY SCOUT DRESS
Spring/summer 1992

Hemingway pokes fun at Baden-Powell with a tongue-in-cheek look at the boy scouts.

Footwear Red or Dead
style: this surreal image
was used as a publicity
flyer. Other unlikely
shoe-wearers in the series
included a table leg and
an elephant's foot.

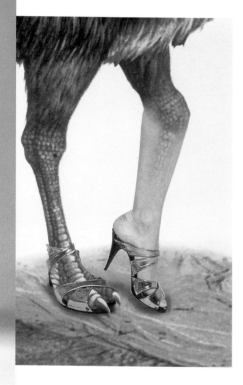

COCKTAIL SKIRT
Spring/summer 1997

Any time, any place,
anywhere . . . this fetching
miniskirt is constructed
entirely from aperitif labels.

"Of course the humor doesn't appeal to everyone, but we can't be everything to everybody. Humor is a selling point for Red or Dead, even if it doesn't work well when it comes to magazine spreads. Most people would prefer to have a smile rather than a grimace on their face. Enjoyment is important: you tend to look for people with a sense of humor, who enjoy life—and clothes can tell you that about someone. For a woman, dressing up like something out of a lads' magazine isn't nearly as attractive as making yourself look human. Fashion can make you inhuman, but humor can make clothes human again.

"I loved the 'Geography Teacher' collection. We wanted to get across the way that often the coolest people in the world are those who are the most uncool, and geography teachers embody that for me. It was a really witty collection. Things like the map print, taking styles and fabrics that would be classed as unwearable—corduroy, plus fours [knickerbockers], geeky specs, dodgy tattersalls and shirts—all the clothes that my geography teacher wore. And, of course, beards; I even grew a beard myself for that collection. It looked incredibly ugly, but it fitted in with the overall feel.

"GEOGRAPHY TEACHER" COLLECTION
Fall/winter 1997

Not all beards and plus fours [knickerbockers], the "Geography Teacher" collection also featured prim-but-sexy womenswear.

"GEOGRAPHY TEACHER" COLLECTION
Fall/winter 1997

Making the uncool cool, Hemingway explores the mysteries of his old geography teacher's fashion sense by playing on corduroy, tank tops [vests], and lurid print shirts.

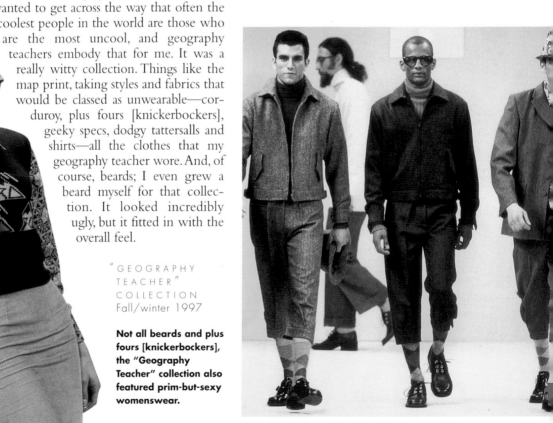

28

PEACOCK SHOWGIRL
Fall/winter 1994

**The Folies-Bergère come to town
with what Hemingway calls his
"posh call girl" outfit, creating an
uplifting finale to the otherwise
sober "Keyhole" collection.**

"We like to put on a 'show,' it's a great way to get the Red or Dead message across. It's got to make a statement. We sent Amanda de Cadenet down the catwalk with a poodle, and Sky TV weatherman Francis Wilson in a glitter suit and Elvis quiff; that was kitsch. It's so much better than having Kate Moss on the catwalk. It's like saying, 'Get real.'

"We also poked fun at the whole 'supermodel' concept, by finding Naomi Campbell's mum. Nobody had heard of her then, and we got loads of publicity. It was the same with the Shirley Bassey lookalike who sang 'Hey Big Spender!' at the end of a show. She was unbelievably good, and people thought she was the real thing. Another catwalk was staged on a platform floating in a swimming pool; we did it like a sad Miss World type of show. There was synchronized swimming with models parading up and down, and Ruth Madoc from [British sitcom] Hi-De-Hi compèring [emceeing].

"I see the catwalk as a necessary evil. It's not hard to work out what the press want. If you put breasts on the catwalk, they'll put the picture on the cover. The spring/summer 1998 collection was the first time we didn't show any flesh, and we got no front covers. It was very well thought-out, the most intelligent catwalk show we'd ever done, but it didn't get the pictures. You could do the worst stuff you've ever dreamed of, and as long as it's got something outrageous in it, you'll get the press coverage.

"There was a time when we didn't draw the line correctly between the kitsch and the wearable. For the Liberace collection, in 1991, the fashion was terrible; we fell into the trap of erring on the side of the ridiculous. Then there was the teddy bear idea for fall/winter 1995: it was only part of the show, and the rest worked, but the teddy print was so rude. We had cute teddies buggering each other, teddies giving oral sex—I think we went too far on that one.

"Having been brought up in a house full of kitsch, I find it's one of the few art forms that inspire me. Maybe that's because it's the only kind of working-class art. It's achievable—anybody can get into kitsch art. Car-boot art, thrift art, bad art, sad art, or whatever you want to call it: everybody can access it. Anyway, who's to say what's good or bad taste?"

SHOWSTOPPERS
1995 and 1996

Hemingway's love–hate relationship with the press does not stop him from putting on a good show. Catwalk highlights have included a Shirley Bassey lookalike *(top left)*, TV presenter Amanda de Cadenet *(left)*, and Naomi Campbell's mother *(right)*, who provided an ironic take on the cult of the supermodel.

Ruth Madoc, of the British TV sitcom *Hi-De-Hi*, joins the models for a camped-up commentary during the spring/summer 1994 catwalk. "Miss World" tiara meets bridal veil for the kitsch finale *(far left)*.

TEDDY BEAR PRINT
Fall/winter 1995

Red or Dead may have gone too far with its reworking of teddy bear prints, says Hemingway. For the catwalk show, the rude teddy also appeared on the back of tight satin shorts.

RED OR DEAD has often been accused by the media of deliberate and cynical shock tactics, creating provocatively sick images guaranteed to get the label plenty of publicity. But this is not so, according to Hemingway.

"People are often too quick to be outraged. Most of the collections—in particular the 'New York Dolls' show, which caused such a fuss—have a specific reason behind the imagery. To me, that collection was more political than sick. Because there were knives and blood on the catwalk, people found it distasteful, but it was the general mood at the time. *Dazed and Confused* [the British cult style magazine] had a shoot with knives and blood around this time, and suddenly there were bits of meat all over the place. People were bored; it was the start of a reaction against all those 'nice' fashion shoots. At Red or Dead we've always avoided pretty fashion shots, and the idea of using shock tactics, such as dwarfs on the catwalk, came from that, from wanting to challenge the fashion industry's beauty values.

"I don't think I've set out to upset people by using sick images. But I've always thought, well, if people don't get the point, then that's their problem. I've always liked pushing back the boundaries of taste, seeing how far you can go, just for the hell of it. I like to look at notions of what is political and what is bad taste, and then play around with them.

DWARFS ON THE CATWALK
Fall/winter 1995

Putting dwarfs on the catwalk was, for Hemingway, a way of challenging the fashion industry's beauty values.

4 REAL
Spring/summer 1996

Part of the "New York Dolls" collection, the "4 Real" bodypaint was a reference to singer Richey of the Manic Street Preachers, who, when asked by a journalist if his band was for real, carved the words deep into his own skin.

"NEW YORK
DOLLS"
COLLECTION
Spring/summer 1996

**With knives and blood
on the catwalk, the
spring/summer 1996
show caused a storm of
controversy and was
dubbed "A Bloody
Disgrace" by the British
tabloid press.**

he sick face of
ritish fashion

"The 'New York Dolls' catwalk was actually an anti-nuclear protest. The thinking behind the show was, what could happen if one of those bombs went off? If there were a nuclear explosion, how would bored housewives react to their soaps not being on TV? It was just a bit of theater on the catwalk; in fact we had already designed the clothes, but the next day we were labeled 'The sick face of British fashion.' People were camping out on my doorstep and interviewing my two daughters.

"I'm a great believer in challenging accepted values. That's one of the reasons why we don't only use models on our catwalk, we also use normal people—including some who many might call pig ugly. The fashion press may call this sick, but we want fashion to be accessible to everyone. It's about breaking down the barriers, not just of fashion, but of beauty, as well.

"I'm quite proud of the fact that, when it comes to the launch of a film that's got lots of street appeal, the film companies ask us to join in. We were the only fashion company that got involved in promoting *Pulp Fiction* and *Trainspotting*; we did official T-shirts for both films. We even reconstructed the 'dirtiest toilet in Scotland' scene from *Trainspotting* for our shop windows—complete with fake vomit and used condoms. The police raided our Nottingham shop; they said the window display was distasteful and closed down the shop on a Saturday afternoon. The publicity was great, especially as we didn't think that would happen in a million years.

"The same thing happened when *The Full Monty* was released. We were asked to promote the film, so we held stripping competitions in each of the shops. An officer from the Nottingham vice squad spent the whole day in our shop trying to stop people from going 'too far.' Maybe it's something in the water up there which makes them more prudish."

BIKER MODEL
Spring/summer 1995

For one show, Red or Dead asked some of their motorcycle couriers to be models. The result was about as far removed as could be from the stylized beauty of traditional catwalks.

TRAINSPOTTING TOILET
1996

To mark the opening of the cult movie *Trainspotting*, Red or Dead recreated the infamous "dirtiest toilet in Scotland" scene— down to the last detail.

"NEW YORK DOLLS"
COLLECTION
Spring/summer 1996

Models wore gas masks to reflect the anti-nuclear theme of the controversial spring/summer 1996 collection.

HEMINGWAY IS HAPPY to use Red or Dead as a soapbox to highlight political issues close to his heart. His association with the environmental pressure group Greenpeace goes back many years, and his strong anti-fur-trade stance has made him one of the most outspoken supporters of the charity Lynx (Respect for Animals). Hemingway's political convictions reflect the politics of youth culture: if you object to something, use every means at your disposal to shout about it.

"I've been brought up always to question things. It's especially important for young people to do this because the day that youth culture agrees with the government—even if the government is 100 percent right in everything—is the day there will be no youth culture. Out of disagreement and out of questioning come change and new ideas. It worries me that [British Prime Minister] Tony Blair is now trying to hijack youth culture, because it's just going to backfire on him.

"We encouraged everyone to give money to Greenpeace before one of our catwalk shows. This caused all sorts of problems because the fashion press resented paying to see a show. But since they were giving money to a good cause, they dared not say no. At the time, Greenpeace was protesting against French nuclear testing in the South Pacific. I could hardly believe that nuclear testing was still going on. We thought we'd do something about it, so on either side of the catwalk we had big French flags saying 'Non.'

"Sometimes we've done something for the right reasons and it has been misread. We did a print called Guru, which showed all the different religious gurus together—Muslims, Sikhs, and others side by side—and nearly ended up with a fatwa on our hands. It started with a guy going into the Nottingham store (Nottingham again!) with one of those big ceremonial Sikh machetes, waving it around and shouting that the print was demeaning to his religion. Every day we got a sackful of protesting letters. I suppose it was naive to think that we could show all religions working in harmony, but we didn't think it would cause so much trouble. Eventually, we withdrew the print from the shops, because we did come to believe that we were insulting people; I was also worried that somebody was going to get hurt.

"A lot of design ideas can come from news stories. The 'Sucky Fucky Love You Long Time' printed dress came from a press article about the Far East sex trade. It's about the way Westerners go over there as sex tourists, but never tell anyone at home. The dresses were throwing it back in their faces. Another cause that we took up was the coal miners—this was in 1993, when

"NON"
Spring/summer 1996

Hemingway has never been afraid to use the catwalk as a political vehicle. Appalled by French nuclear testing in the South Pacific, he teamed up with activist group Greenpeace to get his message across.

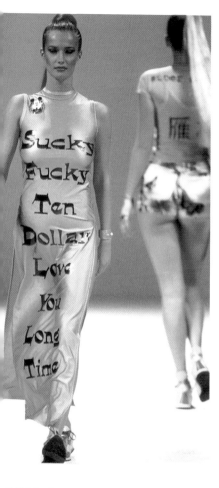

UCKY FUCKY
pring/summer 1995

GURU PRINT
Fall/winter 1997

his sheaf dress resulted
rom Hemingway's
disgust at tourists who
xploit the Far East's
ex industry. He saw it
is a way of throwing
heir hypocrisy back in
heir faces.

Avoiding a fatwa, but
only just, Red or
Dead's infamous Guru
print showed different
religious figures side
by side. The print had
to be withdrawn
after protests.

Expressing a concern for the environment does not mean toning down the flamboyant Red or Dead style. Thi intricate dress is made from ecologically friendly fibers such as linen and cotton.

the Tories [the Conservative government] were in the process of killing off the mining industry (I'm from a mining family). We had a T-shirt that said 'Mine,' a play on words, of course, and the collection was big on workwear, with lots of heavy leather. They looked like old miners' clothes. It was quite clever and tongue-in-cheek, but there was also a serious message behind it.

"I think our tie-up with prison workers sums up our political stance more than anything else does. A high-security jail sent an invitation to all the designers on the British Fashion Council's list, asking them to a prison catwalk show. We thought, 'This is interesting, why

"SHOPPING" DRESS
Spring/summer 1991

In a timely comment on the "shop until you drop" consumer society that had become endemic by the early 1990s, this dress is made from discarded product wrappers. While it makes a strong ecological point, there is a touch of irony in the fact that it was first seen on the ultimate consumer vehicle: the fashion catwalk.

"ANIMALS"
COLLECTION
Fall/winter 1990

The catwalk model clutching a lamb—and wearing Red or Dead's controversial straw dress—was an obvious pastiche of one of British Prime Minister Margaret Thatcher's publicity stunts.

39

not?'—but we went without an agenda. Prisoners had made their own collections, most of which were absolutely awful. No designers apart from ourselves turned up and I thought, 'Well that's a good sign, it must be right for Red or Dead if no one else is doing it.' We talked to the prison governors and they said, 'We've got all these facilities, we've set up a production unit, and we could manufacture for you.' Red or Dead was doing its own workwear collection, and we thought, 'Blooming heck, authentic workwear—opportunity knocks!'

"We considered the issues carefully. It's in our mission statement to have enlightened values, and so we wondered whether it was enlightened to employ rapists and murderers to make our clothes. We weighed up the pros and cons and decided that just because somebody has done something wrong, it doesn't mean that they can't be given an interest and some training for the outside world. We predicted that there would be a lot of criticism, that people would say we were exploiting prisoners. So we paid factory rates and worked out a deal with the prison whereby the money went towards the running of the prison, with the prisoners only getting a nominal payment.

"We got slammed by some of the press for giving work to murderers. So we called a press conference, which was really well attended—even CNN turned up. The American coverage turned out to be the most enlightened. The next thing we knew the same system was being trialed in the U.S.—where it's still going strong.

"We've had our share of criticism, but as long as some people understand the political message, then I think it's all right. There is nothing I wish I hadn't said. But, with hindsight, I think that maybe I haven't done Red or Dead any favors by not schmoozing more with the press. If I had been less critical of journalists in the past, then they might not have spent their entire time misinterpreting Red or Dead's political message."

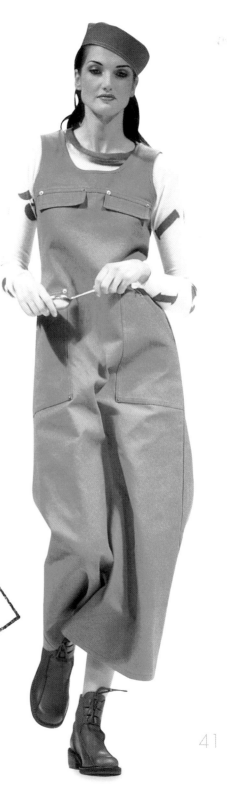

Teaming up with high-security prisoners to produce a collection provoked press criticism, but the system has now become established practice in the U.S. Hemingway capitalized on the prison image by using motifs such as arrows and prison numbers, and making stylistic references to utilitarian workwear.

WHILE HEMINGWAY's political stance and visual jokes attract most of the attention, there is an altogether less complicated influence on Red or Dead's designs—summed up by the word "nice." Within Red or Dead's design ethos, things don't always have to be dipped in meaning and symbolism; the simple pleasures of life have acted as a catalyst for some of the label's most popular designs.

"It's not all politics and shock tactics—there is a more acceptable side to Red or Dead as well. We have done some clothes that people find desirable on a really simple level, believe it or not. At the end of the day you've got to make money, you've got to sell clothes. If everything were political and hard-hitting, it would be just too exhausting—for us to design, and for our customers as well.

"Sometimes, people just want to look nice, sometimes I want to look nice; it doesn't need to be any more complicated than that. I like a varied life. Sometimes you just want things to be nice. I got married and it was nice! I really don't think you can be cynical all the time.

SILK-LEAF HAT
Fall/winter 1993

One of Red or Dead's more elaborate catwalk stunts, the spherical hat is made from hundreds of silk leaves.

TCHECHNIKOV DRESS
Fall/winter 1994

Red or Dead experiments with purely decorative treatments, playing with feather trims for a sophisticated look.

WEDDING DRESS
Spring/summer 1993

The finale to the "Russian Doll" catwalk collection follows Hemingway's take on marriage as being "nice."

LOVE HEART
PRINT
Spring/summer
1991

Prints are a strong element in all of Red or Dead's collections, and the "naughty but nice" Love Heart design is one of Hemingway's favorites.

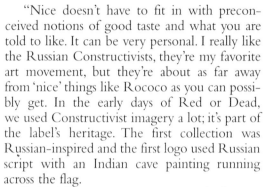

"Nice doesn't have to fit in with preconceived notions of good taste and what you are told to like. It can be very personal. I really like the Russian Constructivists, they're my favorite art movement, but they're about as far away from 'nice' things like Rococo as you can possibly get. In the early days of Red or Dead, we used Constructivist imagery a lot; it's part of the label's heritage. The first collection was Russian-inspired and the first logo used Russian script with an Indian cave painting running across the flag.

"The fish print was nice; so were the butterflies; the love heart was niceness with a twist of rudeness; the Russian dolls were nice. The sunflowers are lovely; they're just nice because they sum up summer. It's not complicated or deep, it's just quite nice to say, 'It's just nice,' and use the word nice about a hundred times. I think being nice is very underrated. There's one thing

"RUSSIAN DOLL"
COLLECTION
Spring/summer 1993

Graduating babushka models wear the Russian Doll print, embodying the lighter side of Red or Dead.

RED HERRING PRINT
Fall/winter 1992

Not all Red or Dead designs need to carry a message; some are chosen purely for their visual impact. The quirky fish print found its way onto a variety of designs, including a voluminous floaty dress.

SUNFLOWER PRINT
Spring/summer 1994

Evoking a bright summer's day, the Sunflower print *(opposite)* is used to enhance sophisticated eveningwear.

you have to be in this company—apart from talented, of course: you have to be nice. You can take the piss [make fun], be ironic, you can play practical jokes, but if at the end of the day you're not nice to everybody you meet, you're out. A human being is supposed to have certain values. Loads of designers are inhuman; a lot of them think that they are gods and that they can ride roughshod over everyone they meet. But everybody involved with Red or Dead has to be human and nice to everybody.

"Nice things are really important. If somebody is happy when they're reading something or looking at something, or wearing something, then it's great. People do remember the happy times in their lives rather than the sad times. And clothes can be a really positive trigger."

SILK CHIFFON
DRESSES
Fall/winter 1997

These semi-transparent textures are extremely wearable, and quite restrained by Red or Dead's standards.

CATWALK
FINALE
Fall/winter 1993

The accent on Red or Dead catwalks is to have a good time, evident from the smiling faces at the end of the show.

GOLD LAMÉ DRESS
Fall/winter 1994

Fluid and slinky lines, with an almost 1930s air, give this sheaf dress a classic and timeless feel not always associated with the label.

RUSSIAN DOLL HAT
Spring/summer 1993

Another one of Red or Dead's catwalk extravaganzas, this striking cartwheel-sized hat formed part of the show's finale.

FRINGED DRESS
Spring/summer 1998

Once again Hemingway proves that Red or Dead is more than capable of producing "nice" clothes without a message.

The future

RED OR DEAD has always looked forward, never back, with Hemingway quick to embrace change of all sorts. He does not believe that getting older will make it harder for him to understand the youth market that lies at the core of his business. On the contrary, he is relaxed and confident about the continued success of Red or Dead.

"It definitely becomes easier as you get older. It's amazing how cyclical fashion is, and now we are seeing things come round all over again. I don't see Red or Dead going all futuristic with the new millennium. I think that look has very limited appeal, and we've already done it anyway. You can only design so many futuristic things, because people don't want to go around looking like extras from *Star Trek*. Kids just don't want to look like Klingons, I'm afraid.

"Fabric will be a really important development for Red or Dead. After all, you can't change the shape of the human body, not radically, anyway. Designers who do end up with collections that nobody wants to wear. What you can do is play with the look of a garment, and also the feel. You can do a lot with fabric. It can be through technology—for example, the development of synthetic footwear materials with the properties of leather. The manufacturers are already there in terms of the material 'breathing' like leather, and in the way it works with your foot; now it's just a matter of getting the price down. It can also be through print— Red or Dead is well known for its original prints, and that's going to continue in the future.

"I like new things. That's the best thing about humanity, the way we can move forward. I want Red or Dead to be part of the future. We run a mighty fine Web site, which was one of the first fashion sites. It's very witty, it's very entertaining, it's got naked men. People really like it—we get loads of feedback. I think it appeals because we are not afraid to take the piss

"FUTURE SKI" BODYSUITS Fall/winter 1995

Hemingway has always embraced the future, and Red or Dead's collections often reveal his impatience with getting on to the next idea. He has also played with futuristic images, from the early Space Baby collection to clinging bodysuits.

The archetypal biker's
jacket is redefined
with a futuristic
silhouette and almost
metallic sheen.

"AVANT-GARDE"
BODYSUIT
Spring/summer 1996

Shades of the film
Barbarella abound in
this space-age catwalk
look, complete with
waspy waist and
matching boots.

49

out of [make fun of] ourselves, which makes the whole thing really approachable. Our Web site very much reflects the Red or Dead values. We really want to demystify fashion, to make it an exciting thing that people won't be turned off from or frightened by. Fashion can be very unapproachable, and Red or Dead will continue to change that with all the technology available.

"People might think Red or Dead are confrontational and aggressive, but we're not. I'm not. That's far too simplistic a take on our philosophy. Sometimes Red or Dead designs are about celebrating the simpler pleasures in life. There have been many really positive influences on the label as well. I'm a family man with four kids who just happens to believe there are other ways of looking at things. To understand Red or Dead, you need to understand that. By turning things on their heads, by looking to politics instead of the history of art, and by finding inspiration in everyday life, you can come up with a new perspective, a fresh approach, which gets your message across far more effectively."

RED OR DEAD
WEB SITE
Launched September 1997

The core values of Red or Dead—to make fashion fun, approachable, and affordable—are reflected in Red or Dead's innovative Web site (www.redordead.co.uk). The site, which changes regularly, has included a male striptease quiz and a spoof love story, as well as up-to-the minute shots from catwalk shows.

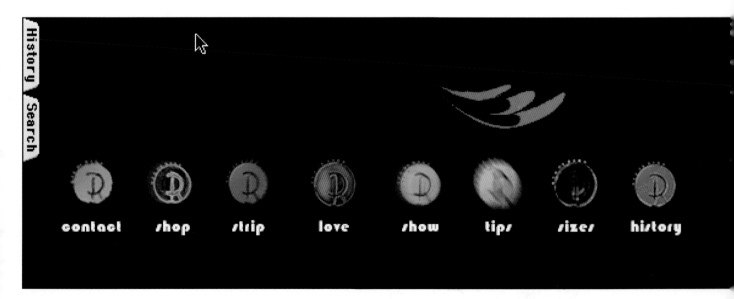

Forward Stop Refresh Home Search Mail Favorites Larger Smaller Preferences

Address: http://www.redordead.co.uk/contact.html

Best of the Web   Today's Links   Web Gallery   Product News   Microsoft   Office for Macintosh

To open sit here

BY E-MAIL
*par la poste
electronique*

CONTACTS & COMMENTS LONDON

1st

Tell us what you think of our website, our products and the Red or Dead brand. The best complaint as well as the most praising letter will win a Red or Dead Internet T-shirt.
Also design a Red or Dead T-shirt, the

41-44 Neal St
Covent Garden
London WC2

14 Caxtongate
Cannon Street
Birmingham B1

35 King Street
Manchester
M1

8 Eldon Court
Devonshire Quarter
Sheffield
S1 4GY

38a
Kensington High St
Kensington
London W8

3-4 Princess Sq
Newcastle
NE1 8EG

14 Cheapside
Nottingham
NG1 2HU

Your Name
Your Email

Submit Reset

View Recent Comm

wayne's scratch'n'sniff page

Back Refresh Search Mail Favorites Larger Smaller Preferences

Address: http://www.redordead.co.uk/scratchfrane.html

Best of the Web Today's Links Web Gallery Product News Microsoft Office for Macintosh

Red or Dead Love Stories

Welcome to the Red or Dead on-line Love Story.
For those of you who have just joined us, the story
has been running for three passion packed episodes.

Part 1
The Separatists of Love

Part 2
Love Reigns Supreme

Part 3
Love on the Rocks

LOVE ON
THE ROCKS
EPISODE 3

Thumbs up.
Very fruity.

To fully utilise this section you will require
Macromedia's latest Flash plug-in.

Sizing Charts

contact

Women   *Men*   *& Shoes*

BY E-MAIL
*par la poste
electronique*

CONTACTS & COMMENTS

1st

Chronology

1961
Wayne born in Morecambe, Lancashire, England.

1961
Gerardine born in Padiham, Lancashire.

1966
England wins World Cup.

1976
Punk.

1977
The Buzzcocks.

1981
Wayne and Gerardine meet in a disco; love blossoms.

1982
Wayne and Gerardine empty their wardrobes onto a small market stall in Camden, London. By the end of the year there are 16 stalls, with shipments of secondhand clothing and footwear being brought in from all over the world.

1983
Outlet in Kensington opens selling clothes designed and made by Gerardine.

First Red or Dead collection, inspired by Russian peasant clothing, is an immediate success, with large orders from Macy's. Small production unit and first-ever Red or Dead shop open in Blackburn, Lancashire. Red or Dead becomes first retailer to sell Dr. Martens workwear shoes as a fashion item.

1984
Footwear becomes a major force at Red or Dead—at first, old stock of 1950s and 1960s canvas, then canvas sourced from the Far East.

1985
Stores open in Camden and Manchester, selling a mixture of early Red or Dead clothing, secondhand clothing, retro canvas, and Dr. Martens.

1986
Jack Hemingway born. Store opens in London's Soho, selling the first Red or Dead footwear range designed by Wayne and Gerardine.

1987
Tilly Hemingway born. Store opens in Neal Street, Covent Garden. Regular lines outside the shop due to the success of the "Watch shoe," as sported by teen band Bros.

1988
Business expands and the building of a design team begins.

1989
First catwalk collection, "Space Baby" (for spring/summer 1990), is shown to worldwide acclaim.

1990
Corey Hemingway born. Spring/summer collection: "Space Baby." Fall/winter collection: "Animals."

1991
Stores open in Copenhagen, Birmingham, and London's Kensington. Spring/summer collection: "Shopping." Fall/winter collection: "Liberace."

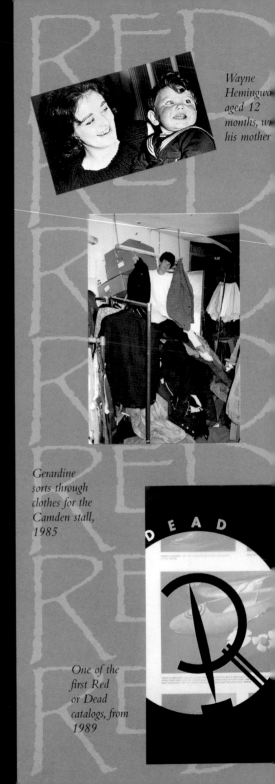

Wayne Hemingway aged 12 months, with his mother

Gerardine sorts through clothes for the Camden stall, 1985

One of the first Red or Dead catalogs, from 1989

Red or Dead
catalog, 1991

The Kensington
High Street
store, opened
in 1991

REDORDE

Men's brogue,
1987

1992
Store opens in Leeds.
Begin work on the
concept of Dr.
Martens clothing.
Spring/summer
collection: "Mad in
England." Fall/winter
collection: "Spy."

1993
Further U.K. stores
open, including
Thomas Neals in
Covent Garden. Sign
contract to be the first
designer shoe
company to advise
Marks & Spencer
[British clothes stores].
Spring/summer
collection: "Russian
Doll." Fall/winter
collection: "Skeleton."

Red or Dead
catalog, 1992

Gurner print jacket
and loveheart bag,
1992

Subtle Red or Dead promotional
image, 1992

Gurner print, from "Mad in England," 1992

Tartan Dr. Martens, 1992

Spring/summer 1993

Red or Dead
BRITISH PASSPORT

AUTUMN/WINTER
1992/1993

Invitation to "Spy" collection, 1992

Invitation to spring/summer 1992 collection

Red or Dead catalog, 1993

Fall/winter 1993

1994

Store opens in Tokyo. Launch of Dead Basic diffusion range. Spring/summer collection: "Sunflower." Fall/winter collection: "Keyhole."

1995

Win the British Fashion Council's inaugural Street Style Designer of the Year award. Wayne and Gerardine sell to Facia group. Spring/summer collection: "Butterfly." Fall/winter collection: "Ski."

Red or Dead catalog, 1994

Fall/winter 1994

Invitation to fall/winter 1995 collection

Spring/summer 1995

Change of address card, 1994

Spring/summer 1995

Red or Dead catalog, 1994

Fall/winter 1995

57

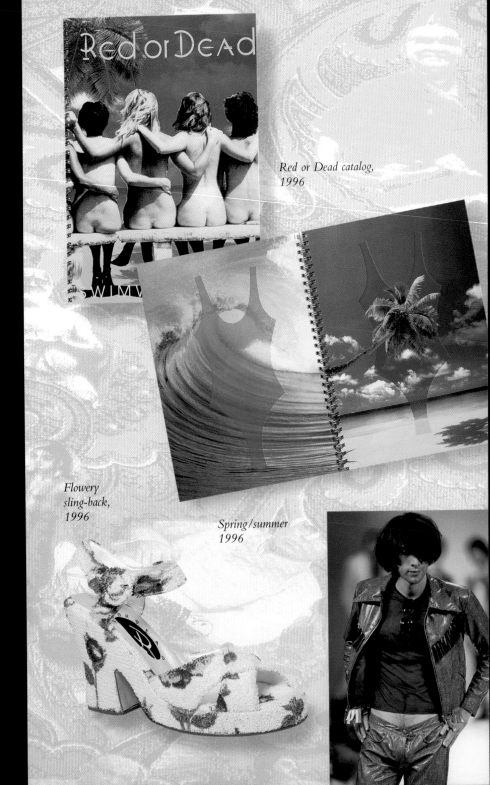

1996
Facia collapses; Wayne and Gerardine buy back Red or Dead in a joint venture with The Pentland Group. Win the British Fashion Council's Street Style Designer of the Year award for the second time. Spring/summer collection: "New York Dolls." Fall/ winter collection: "Ism."

1997
Beck Hemingway born. Win Street Style Designer of the Year award for the third time. Spring/summer collection: "Indian Summer." Fall/ winter collection: "Geography Teacher."

Red or Dead catalog, 1996

Flowery sling-back, 1996

Spring/summer 1996

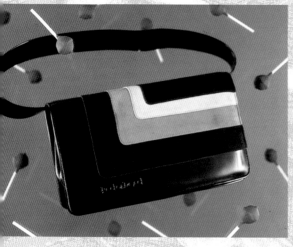

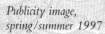

*Publicity image,
spring/summer 1997*

*Publicity image,
fall/winter 1996*

Platform mule, 1997

*Invitation to
fall/winter
1997 collection*

Fall/winter 1996

1998
Stores open
in Prague and Tokyo.
Spring/summer
collection: "Beautiful
Freaks." Fall/
winter collection:
"A Road Movie
Across the States."

*Montaged publicity image,
1998*

*Red or Dead
spectacles flyer,
1998*

Spring/summer 1998

Spring/summer 1998

Spring/summer 1998

Spring/summer 1998

Red or Dead point-of-sale, 1998

Fall/winter 1998

Index

Acknowledgments

The publishers wish to thank Wayne Hemingway, Gerardine Hemingway, and Chris Wood for their kind assistance with all aspects of this book.

Photographic credits
Guy Ryecart: pages 5, 11, 12 middle, 18, 19, 25 top, 53 bottom right, 58 bottom left, 59 middle right.
All other photographs courtesy Red or Dead. Catwalk photographers: Suresh Karadia and Chris Moore.

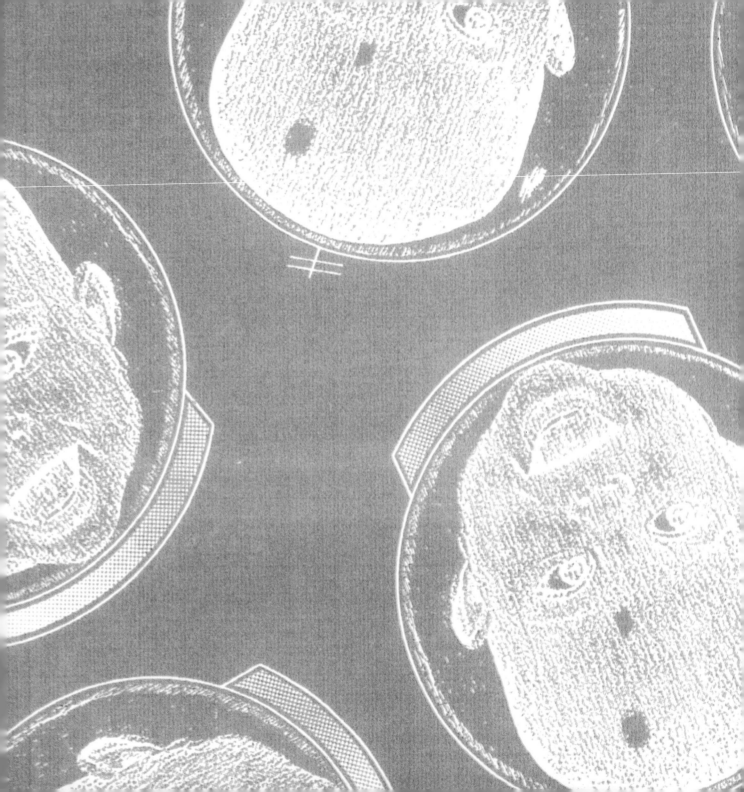